This is dedicated to tomorrow
in spite of yesterday.

Also by SJ Duncan

Novels

Bash
One in the Barrelhouse

Collected Poems

Like a Fire Praying for Rain
Three Rights and a Left
The Long Dark Lonesome

Three
Rights
And
A
Left

SJ
Duncan

Ink Ribbon Press

First Ink Ribbon Press trade paperback edition: 2014

For information about the author visit

www.sjduncan.com

Ink Ribbon Press is a division of Ink Ribbon Publishing. For information about bulk purchasing, events, or appearances, contact Ink Ribbon Press at

www.inkribbonpress.com

ISBN: 0615856446

ISBN-13: 978-0615856445

Contents

Part I – Some of the Same Old Habits

Part II – The Rights

Part III – The Left

Part I
Some of the
Same Old Habits

A Ladder and a Roof

At two AM
the old man
took the ladder from the garage
and climbed up to the roof
he never said why
but if you ask his daughter
she'll tell you
he hadn't been the same
since his wife died
and then there was the war
he never talked about
and the failed business
and some health problems
and when you add it all together
you begin to see
why an old man
with nothing but
a ladder and a roof
would choose to jump
at two AM.

He lived
but he was never the same
and he never walked again
and the only thing he ever said about it
was that if he'd been a more successful man
he would've had a taller house
to jump from.

Camp

The girl and I made camp
by the side of the road
cooked some beans
and hunkered down

There were headlights moving
in the distance
and the two of us
tried to snuggle for warmth
but couldn't stop arguing over
knees and elbows
cold feet
and who was getting
most of the blanket
so we called it quits
and went our separate ways
in the dead of night.

It would have been warmer
to just get along
bite our tongues
and each other's lips
but that's not what we did.

What we did
was spend a cold and lonely night
by ourselves
on opposite sides of the road.

Seaside

we sit by the ocean
the wind comes in
with the smell of salt
there are a million things
down there
in the blue dark
we hold hands
we don't talk
there are a million things
down there
in the blue dark

some of them bite

45 Poems About Coffee and Time

My life story is called
45 Poems About Coffee and Time.
When the movie came out
watching it alone
became the thing to do.
Social media
never recognizes you
for the genius you are.
We spent Saturday
posting selfies
by the lake.
Each year
we add a thousand new words
to our vocabulary
and forget just as many.
The poems reached critical mass
one day
and had to be contained.
I put them in a book
and called it
One Hundred Thousand Ticks of the Clock.
My patience is wearing thin.
My preference
is that I get to keep doing this
forever.
We'll call that book
A Million Years in America.
We won't stop
until we can't go on.
Night time is the right time
but morning time is my warning time
and I'm telling you

to keep your eyes on the road.

Four Million Poems
About Falling Down Holes
is a heavy load.

The Sound of Industry

They make the house more bearable
these old typewriters
collected from wherever they've been
these last fifty or sixty or eighty
or a hundred years
machines of loving grace
I've heard them called.

We had one when I was a kid
a big, heavy black one
and as soon as they taught me to spell
I started teaching myself to write
on that big, heavy machine
sitting in my room for hours
stringing words
my first love
my oldest flame.

I love the sound they make.
It's the sound of industry.
It's the sound of riveting yourself
back together
each time you start to fall apart.

Sometimes I find them at yard sales
and antique shops
and sometimes I get a good deal
and when I find one
I bring it home
and clean it up
gun oil and elbow grease
little gears

and rods
and keys
and hammers
clacking
like a
racked pistol.

I type.
I listen.

It's the sound of a swift
clean
and efficient
exorcism.

I still sit in my room for hours
stringing words
and when the house gets too quiet
I roll in a clean sheet of paper
and beat back the loneliness
one key-stroke at a time.

They help make the house more bearable
that way
like lamps and nightlights
background noise
faithful dogs
and warm thoughts
of old flames.

Burrito

Made a list of the bills
we're overdrawing again
right back in the hole we were in
*how did I spend so much money
in such* short order cooks
know me by plate
cravings
ordering the same damn thing
every time I sit down
at the same damn place
ruts
and sluts
bring me a coffee
bring me some desert
what would it hurt
to spend a little time together
she doesn't know
I don't know
and neither of us cares
money money money
wouldn't be such a problem
if I had someone
to keep track of it for me
that's the answer
but at this moment
there's no money to keep track of
so this whole line of thought
becomes a joke on me
scrounge up enough coins
for a burrito
and have a little pity
for the ones who have it easy.

Marching Right Along

I face impossible odds.
I don't know what's up
or what time it is.
I don't know my limits.
I continue on unbeaten paths
throwing coins in wishing wells
and if this were a lottery
I would spend every last dollar
on chances.
I don't know enough to know
when enough is enough.
I bet it all on myself
but the dice are suspended
in mid-air.
I go all in.
I go all out.
I simply go
and I don't care about the odds.
I don't even care
that poetry is dead
and poets die early.
I have to do this anyway.

Child of the '90s

Child of the '90s
taught to hate himself
by people
who hated themselves
sick
degenerate
misfits
with very large megaphones
earworms
hooks and grooves
lyrical mumblings
and spiritual fumblings
this poor child of the '90s
hating everything and everyone
convinced
that it wasn't cool
or in his nature
to
be
happy.

The Old Beast

The old beast
can't seem to stay down for long
perched on a limb
eyeing the scene
hopping down at the slightest sound
or inclination
that something may be going on
and when something is
or even when it isn't
he can't keep himself
from running over
and pawing the young beast to the ground
just so the young beast knows
who was here first
and who runs this cage.

The young beast cowers.

He hasn't yet realized
that he is bigger than the old beast.

Changes

Sold the house
moved into an apartment
just off the loop
close to a burger place
a coffee shop, too,
and just down from a bookstore
and near half the people I love
and not too far from the other half.

(Continuing on my journey
of growth and personal development
gradually becoming
something
or perhaps just
myself)

I have no time for
fixing mistakes in the rough draft

I let them lie
as they fall
like sleeping dogs on the page
which I'll have to rouse
and shoo out the door later
but right now
I step over them
let them sleep
the guests haven't arrived
and the dogs aren't bothering anything.

I love
with all my heart

and I tend to my task.

Ease
is not too much to ask.

It's just past midnight
and cold outside.
The dogs can sleep inside tonight
on the page where they lie.

I'll sleep here
in this apartment
which is clean
fresh paint
new carpet.

I will not get my deposit back
by the time I'm done.

Too much fun.

Cooking up something good
here in this new place
and the guests will be here soon
tomorrow
by eleven
maybe noon.

Lord, them's a lot of dogs.

Towel Basket

There's no room here
for a towel basket
lightly stained
by seeping imitation vanilla
along with all the other things
tossed into it
during the move
the exodus
the great escape
from the mess
I had made.

These things, these things,
so many of them
crowding out my days
blocking the sunshine
so that my skin sees
only the slightest ray of light
I am a fish
too far down
to feel right
and I'm sure it's the lack
of light
keeping me glued
to my seat.

Somewhere
up there
sunshine glitters
on the ripples
and there has to be a way

back up.

The towel basket
will go in the trash
along with all the other things.

Like it was a Date

I took my dad's truck into town
that day.

He didn't know it.
He knew that I drove it
on the back roads
but the back roads just happened
to lead into town
and so I followed them
to your house.

I picked you up
in my pick-up truck
and we rode
cruising the back roads
at fifteen
not much older
than the Ford Dad drove.

I couldn't wait another year
or even a few months
at fifteen.

At fifteen
it's now or never
convinced you'll die
or the world may end
at any time.

Now or never.

So I took my dad's truck into town

like it was legal
and picked you up
like it was a date.

You smiled at me
like I was a man.

All It Takes

All it takes
to get started
is one letter
one letter then another
another
until you have
one word
(space)
another letter
then another
a few more
(space)
keep at it
keep going
and never mind that voice
that says
you're going to screw this up
the words are wrong
that's a stupid thing to say
nobody will read you
and those that do
will think you're an idiot
drown that voice out
with the sound
of your own typing
crank it up
loud and fast
drink lots of coffee
smoke 'em if you got 'em
bombs away
and damn the torpedoes.

Get started
keep going
and learn to ignore
all the other stuff.

That's how you do this.

Talk

The phone rings
but I
ignore
snore
sofa to the floor
look up
to see the sun shining
while the phone is ringing
and I'm not sure I want this anymore.

Either a bill collector
or a girl
neither of whom
I want to whirl
with
leave me alone
pull the blanket down
from the couch
and drown the world out.

Coffee coffee
shower
dress
brush
hair and teeth.

Pull
on
your
shoes
and tie
them.

Headed out
in my daily best
which isn't much to brag about
so don't get it confused.

I want it all:
to be
adored
ignored
far away
and back home
from a book tour
all in one breath
and then death
and to never have to do this
anymore.

It was a girl calling.

I don't want to talk right now.

Wondering

You begin to wonder
at the bottom of it
looking up
at where you were before the slip
one bad toehold
and the next thing you know
you're down
at the bottom again
watching the little monkeys
and mountain goats
bubble and bounce
from tree to tree
and rock to rock
as you lie in the gravel
looking up
it wasn't supposed to be this way
yet this is the way it is
one bad toehold
and you never reach the summit
can't even say you made it halfway up

> *we were just getting started*
> *and now we're bust*
> *and our canteens have spilled*
> *in the dust*

one bad toehold
and you begin to wonder
if the universe
is tearing you apart
for a reason.

Down and Out

Feeling
down and out
is not the same as
being
down and out
a little lax on lux
at the moment
no running water
busted ass truck
while the tide licks away
at our sandcastle
but we've been here before
mouths to feed
mouths to feed
you only start talking about mouths to feed
when you start having trouble feeding them
but the thing is
miracles never cease.

Down does not mean out.

Hold on to hope.
Never let them take that
even when they've taken
everything else.

Swallow it
if you have to.

When they're not looking
cough it back up.

When they're not looking
start building again.

When they're not looking
show 'em what you're made of.

Down
does not mean
out.

Chooser

Don't act like
you're doing me a favor
by slipping me your number
and getting indignant
when I don't call
or fall
for you.

I'm not one of these
clambering
stammering
floundering little boys
getting flush-faced
and frenzied
over you.

This is happening
more and more often
and the more I complain about it
the more I get
girls
like you
slipping numbers on napkins
but just so you know
just so it's clear
just so there won't be
any confusion
I am not a beggar.

That means I can be a chooser.

Slip-ups

Slipped
and stabbed myself with a pen
arterial spray
all over the page
for days
should have bled out by now
but
this
thing
craves
more and more
this thing
with no name
no home
and no place to stay
but right here on my shoulder
overseeing
what I'm doing
and so I work
diligently
today
tomorrow
I lay
words
like bricks
brick after brick
building up my tower
and I can already climb
higher
than I ever thought possible
and I can do more
than I ever imagined

and even when I bleed
I'm happy to see
all of this is working out
the way I knew it would.

Cleaning Carpets

Life is funny
that way
you say to yourself
while cleaning carpets
one morning
waiting for the sun to shine
through the windows
so you can see if what you're doing
is doing any good.

You're thinking about her,
that girl from long, long ago
because that's what you do
by yourself
cleaning carpets
in and old house
before dawn.

She has a husband, now,
and kids.

While cleaning carpets
you think of those old days
when the two of you were young
and on fire
and neither of you knew what to do
with the flames.

(So often
we burn ourselves
and blame one another.)

You think about her
because you ran into her
awhile back
and started talking
only talk
but enough talk to be dangerous.

You are free.

She has a husband and kids, now.

You quit talking
because the talk was getting dangerous
but sometimes you think
of sending her a message
a little *how-do-ya-do*
but you know
there's only heartbreak
at the end of that road
for you
or her
or everyone involved.

She has a husband and kids
so you put her out of your head
and you clean your carpets.

After awhile
the sun starts shining through the windows
and finally you see
that what you're doing
is doing some good after all.

Stubborn

I will not obey
or go quietly
about my business
keeping to myself
and hiding my light
from watching eyes
I will not do that
anymore.

It's not that I'm angry
or that I'm not
it's a matter of personal dignity
and self-respect.

As far as I can tell
I own myself
bought me at a pawn shop
cheap
but look at what I've done with me.

I have not obeyed
and I have not gone quietly
about my business
keeping to myself
and hiding my light from watching eyes.

Took me home
polished me up
and set myself apart
from the rest
of the collection.

The rest of the collection
whispers
winces
and twiddles thumbs
but I'm doing things my way
the only way I know how.

Stubborn
is what I am.

Sooner or Later

Slow and steady wins the race
saves face
invites grace
and keeps everything in its proper place.

Sooner or later
she'll want to spend
every evening together.

Slow is smooth
and smooth is fast
the Army friend says.
That's what they taught him
in the Army.

Slow is smooth
and smooth is fast.

We'll see where things go
one day at a time
every other Thursday
every other weekend.

We move slow
but we are smooth
and things are going to get fast.

Sooner or later
we'll want to spend
every evening together.

Smooth is fast

and fast is how things begin to happen
when you realize
that starting out slow
really made things smooth.

Sooner or later
we'll want to buy
a headboard
and a bed skirt.

Four years
you've spent by yourself
crafting this lifestyle
of wallowing in misery
and writing to the world about it.

Four years.

Whiny writer
what will you write about now?

Sooner or later
she'll become your new muse.

Sooner or later
she'll fix everything
that is wrong with you.

Whiny writer
who wants to read about that?

Something Different

When you think
that only
a crazy
person
would do this
at least
you know
you're doing
something
different.

Too Many Distractions Here

I can hear the cats
in the kitchen
where I've shut them up
to get them
to leave me alone.

No kids
this weekend
which means I'm spiraling
drifting
into dark territory
working on the new novel
when I'm not
pacing
making coffee
or cussing at
cats
the phone
the cold
or the same ol' same ol'.

heartburn
headache
brain spasm
migraine
and the ringing in my ears.

Plenty of food
plenty of water
and still, the cats cry.

One of them

managed to open
the fridge.

Who knows how long
it was standing open
in there.

This much is clear:
I need to go where there are no cats.

December of 2012

December of 2012 saw
The Long Dark Lonesome
and the loss of my mind
January came
(cold?)
maybe
I don't remember
but messy
so messy in the house
that we left it that way
and got an apartment
in the city in February
and by March we were rolling
two books out
full steam ahead
April
May
June
July
we were
rocking and rolling
playing shows
and signing books
then August came
some downtime
and down
in my mind
we moved back to the old house
with the ten-foot ceilings
and the single-pane windows
September
I don't remember

October
hurt my side
pain pills
reclined
November
fell off a cliff
December
got back up
grabbed my pen
and got at it again
and here we are
the book money trickles in
in spits and spurts
but money was never the point
anyway
and it seems
that no matter what life throws at me
I
just
can't
quit.

Miner

When you know where gold is
or *think* you do
you get gold fever
it comes on fast
clouds your judgment
makes you do things
like sell your stuff to buy
picks and pans
and leave your wife and kids at home
so you can spend your days digging
and sloshing around
while your nights are spent
tending a campfire
thinking about digging
and sloshing around
and exactly where you might
dig
and slosh around
tomorrow
when the sun comes up
(Oh, how you can't wait
for the sun to come up)
and maybe you hit the mother load
and maybe you go home broke
and maybe you die a lonely old man
lying in bed
thinking of what you lost
for a pan of silt
and a few yellow flakes
that never amounted to much
of anything.

Patience

I'm not impatient
but I get impatient
waiting for all the pieces
to fall into place
waiting for the cement to set
waiting to walk on fresh sidewalks.

I can wait
believe me, I can wait
I've been blessed that way
with an inhuman amount of patience
and the ability to sit idly by
for as long as it takes
yes
yes
I can wait.

The pieces are almost in place
and the cement is firming up
and soon I will
rip down the yellow tape
and when that happens
I won't walk
I'll run.

The Lives We Make

The old man says
we make our lives
either by doing what we want
or not doing what we don't.

People are full of reasons,
he says,
and excuses
and justifications.

For what?
the boy asks.

For living lives they hate,
the old man says.
Little lives sealed up in little boxes,
little lives they hate
the way a dog hates the kennel.
Little lives they love,
the way a kid loves hiding
beneath his blanket.
Little lives lived in little boxes
keeping them safe
from all that space out there,
all that dark space
where anything might be waiting
to grab them.

That's how we live our lives,
he says.
So many of us,
covered from head to toe.

SJ Duncan

The boy tells him
that he is scared of the dark.

The old man laughs.

You're not scared of the dark, he says.
You're scared of all the things
you can't see.
You have to stake your claim
on the possibilities –
all of them:
The possibility
that you might be happy
or devastated
or loved
or lonely
or even the possibility
you might get rich and die
all on the same day.

Once you do that,
he tells the boy,
once you accept the possibility
that anything can happen
and once you realize
you'll still find a way to be alright
you no longer have to live a little life.

The boy thinks about this
and the old man watches him.
The boy won't understand, just yet,
but the seed has been planted,
and the old man is happy.

He wants better for the boy.

He wants the boy
to want better
for himself.

After a while
when they get up to leave
the old man asks the boy,
So, will we make it big or die, today?

I can't wait to find out,
says the boy.

The old man grins,
knowing the boy's life
just got
a little bigger.

Luminous

We are beautiful
luminous
loud
and perfectly flawed
groping in the dark
and stumbling down
blind alleys
trying to find our way.

We are here
for a reason
and purpose
and for such a short season
like so many
cogs and gears
turning inside
this machine
humming
and roaring along.

You will lose your way
as all of us do
from time to time.

Move forward
slowly and carefully
until you find it again.

You'll find it again.

The Box

The box is wooden
engraved with images
of birds and flowers
with a brass latch
and brass hinges.

It came from a store
in the city
years ago
before he knew what he was doing
and at the whim
of what he was feeling.

The box is full of letters
which came in the mail
for her
all those years ago
from him.

Back then,
before the gray
and the wrinkles
and the little pains of living
he wrote her all the time.

He read one of the letters
one day
the other day
and put it back in the box
put the lid on
and set the box on the corner
of the kitchen table

so he could look at it
and feel bad.

He gave her the box
on Valentine's day
all those years ago.

He doesn't count the letters
but guesses
there are a hundred or more.
Silly little letters
from a silly little
love-stricken boy.

At the bottom of the box
he found a few photos.

The boy and girl smiling in them
with their faces pressed together are
so
very
young.

The lid is broken
from a fight they had
many years ago.

He can't remember
which of them
threw the box.

He wonders what
the letters say

but he can't bring himself
to read them.

The people who sold him the box
had no way of knowing
this is what would
become of it:
a broken box
full of letters
she no longer wants
and he can no longer read.

When he is finished
looking at the box
it will go in the closet
way up high.

It may not come down again
in his lifetime.
He's alright with that.

By the End

By the end of it all
there was still the house
the old house with the peeling paint
cracked drywall
and lots of space.

Moving back costs so much
there was no money left
to have the water turned on.

The music stuff
went back in the studio
but like a hole in which the dirt
never sits right again
the stuff didn't sit right
and I couldn't seem to arrange it
so things just went to hell
and I let them.

At a certain point
all you can do is sit back
let it finish crumbling
and then start picking things up.
Again.

I tried to write
but the words wouldn't come
and sitting at a typewriter
with no words
is a bad place to be.

Worse than standing at a sink

with no water.

(We bathed in jug water
warmed on a propane burner
there was no stove
no refrigerator
and we kept our sandwich stuff
in an ice chest –
it all sounds worse than it was.)

After three weeks
of washing and cooking with jugs
we finally had the money
to have the water
turned back on.

When it was on
we threw handfuls of it
into the air
screaming
dancing
stomping the floor
like we had struck oil.

Later
I was able
to have the words turned back on
as well.

Three Poems

I wrote three poems
for you
today.
I don't know if they
are any good
or if they
will make it into the next book
or if I'll decide
later
that they don't adequately represent
myself
my life
the world
our nature
or any of the other things
I try to capture
when I sit at this old desk.

If they do make it in
then I hope you like them
or find some use
for them
and if not
well, then
shove off
because
who asked you
anyway?

They Come Back

They come back
to bite you
don't they
those little lines you wrote
when you were
in the moment
in your prime
pounding it out
and never thinking about
who would read them.

Thought it was a heart attack
that night after the show
when the chest pains went
from bad to worse
and the left arm started going
numb
numb
numb
up the arm
into the chest
into the throat. . .

I'm only thirty-four,
he wrote.

True,
but that's thirty-four years of
fast food
moping
bad mood
self-loathing

and let's not forget all those cigarettes.

Ran to the corner store for some Pall Malls,
he wrote.
Menthols
shorts
he wrote.

Funny how you want to live
when you think you won't.

High blood pressure
is what they said
but in the hospital bed
you think about
all those little lines you wrote
when you felt like *Mr. Invincible,*
Mr. Untouchable,
all those lines about
your own supremacy
throwing them out
and never thinking about
who was going to read them.

In the hospital you think about that.

In the hospital you think,
Sometimes God reads them.

Dominance and Submissions

Allan is a writer. So am I. We both live in the city of Keraway. We both have websites, Facebook pages, Twitter feeds, Instagram; Allen has a bit of a following. So do I.

Why do we do this? Allan asks. Poor bastard.

I know why we do it. I want to tell him, but I don't. What I tell him is this: *We do this because we love it. The words, the craft, the details, the little dramas.* That's what I tell him.

Even though we grew up in the same town, we were never close, never friends. Then we both started publishing and developing our followings. Paths began to cross. Book signings, special events. I've never read his work, but I intend to, someday.

They say imitation is the greatest form of flattery.

About a week after I revamped my website, Allen revamped his. It looks a lot like mine.

One of these days I'm going to be rich, Allan says.

When I get rich I'm gonna get an old school Thunderbird, Allan says.

When I blow up, Keraway's gonna have my name at the city limits on a big ass billboard, Allan says.

I've been at this a lot longer than Allan. Writing, I mean. The notion of getting rich fell off a long time ago. But that's the way it is with dreams. Time, life, circumstance; they're like blades trimming the fat. All the unnecessary hopes, wishes, and fantasies fall away, piece by piece until all you have is the part of the dream that really mattered in the first place, the part that made you start putting words to paper all those years ago. That's where I am, living the new dream. I don't care about the money, or fame, or women, or cars, or being talked about by a million folks I don't know. I have my work, and it keeps me sane, and I'm happy with it.

When I get rich, Allan says, *I'm going to make it rain in the city of Keraway.*

Allen took an online typing test. He blogged about it on his website. Forty-five words per minute. Seven mistakes. He couldn't get work as a secretary with numbers like that. He doesn't know enough to know that.

I watch him, though. About a week after revamping the website, he started posting selfies. His selfies look a lot like mine: Black and white, angled from the left, shadowed around the edges. Artsy.

He has a pretty wife: Josie. Petite little redhead with a Kate Upton smile. She read one of my books. Then she started showing up at my place at night.

I signed the book for her. I talk to her outside, where it's safe, where we aren't alone behind closed doors.

Josie loves my work. That's what she says. And the pics I post of myself. She says she loves my hair. She calls it my mane. I don't tell her that in the wild the mane is a bluff. It makes the lion look bigger. Males rarely live more than a decade in the wild. There is always a younger one, a fresher one, looking to take their place.

I have a bigger following, but Allan is younger.

Some days I feel old, and fat, and lazy. The words don't come easy, those days.

About a week after posting pics like mine, Allan started growing his hair like mine.

Then he started wearing a hat.

Like mine.

I can see his Facebook feed, and I know he's watching mine. I'm thoughtful when I post. Allan's posts make him sound like a jackass.

Allan thinks the new movie theater is gay.

Allan hates the owners of the mall.

Allan went to Sonic and they screwed up his burger.

Allan thinks he's smarter than his readers.

He has a lot of insecurities. They show.

Still, he gets more likes than me. He's more relatable. He's funny.

He's the younger male, looking to take my place.

I don't tell him to ease up or slow it down. He does more commenting than actual writing any damn way.

You talk too much, I tell him.

LOL, is what I get back. All day, every day.

LOL, LOL, LMAO.

Exclamation mark.

Jackass.

Josie tells me she wants to leave him, that he keeps pushing her away, that she doesn't know what she ever saw in him. *He's a boy*, she says. *I need a man.*

I know why she keeps showing up at my door. She's in quicksand and she knows it and now she wants somebody to pull her out. She looks good, but my hands are busy doing this.

I asked how they got together in the first place. She is clearly above his grade.

She digs the writer thing, she says, standing on my porch with her hands in the pockets of her shorts. She moves closer when she says this. I think to pull her against me, lean down, whisper in her ear that I only want to know one thing: *Am I a better writer than your husband?*

I want to kiss her, but women are trouble and I'm living the dream. I don't have time for girlfriends, wives, divorces. I'm doing something different with my life.

Josie's got legs like two miles of seduction. She smells like something you can't wait to get your mouth on.

Am I better than your husband?

That's all I want to know. One of these days I'll start reading Allan's *Wreckless Planet* series (his spelling, not mine), and then I'll know. Until then, I won't think about lions in the wild, and how there's always a younger, fresher male looking to take your place.

Josie says we should get together sometime. Go for a walk. She says she knows a place.

I tell her I'm a busy guy. And I'm not into married women. Get your life straight, then come see me.

Writing is what I spend my time doing.

Clackity-clack.

This.

Why do we do it? Allan asks.

If you don't know, I can't tell you.

LOL!!!

Allan calls himself Keraway's living legend. He posts this on his website, in his feeds.

Allan Carouth: Keraway's Living Legend!

I'm blessed to know I'm a legend in the making. I'm smart enough to keep my mouth shut about it.

Josie comes over often. She leans up close, suggests we go inside.

Tell me I'm a better writer, I say in those visions where we tumble, clutching, stripping, falling into the apartment, onto the couch. Her lips look soft. Her eyes shine, the eyes of an angel leaning over the edge of her cloud, peering down into my world, trying her damndest to fall.

Allan posts about his wife. *Josie* this, *Josie* that. He posts pictures of their new bed. The headboard is nice, good woodwork, detailed.

This is where the magic is made, he posts. *LOL!!*

I sleep on a mattress on the floor. *When* I sleep. Which isn't often.

Allan changed his background image. It looks a lot like mine.

Josie comes over one morning. She says Allan wants to know who designed my bookmarks and who printed them. I give out bookmarks at my signings. Allan thinks that's a great idea.

When he gets rich, Allan is going to buy a boat and a jet-ski and a lake house.

And if *I* get rich?

Doesn't matter, anymore. I have everything I need. All I want is for Josie to stop coming over. . .

. . .*pulling, clutching, tripping, laughing, falling, falling, falling from the heavens, my little red-haired angel, falling from the heavens to the sofa of man.*

On the way out, afterwards, I would remind her to take her halo. We would search for it. The halo would be gone.

I'm not in the business of other men's wives.

Josie comes over again and again.

Standing outside on the porch, smoking, talking. She gets closer. She brushes a strand of hair away from my face. Lionesses favor the densest, darkest manes. I wonder if we're any different, anything more than animals trying our best to act human.

Allan posts his pictures, talking himself up, bad-mouthing the town that would call him its own should he ever get somewhere, get known, get *big*.

I brought you something, Josie says one night.

It's a copy of Allan's newest book. *Wreckless Planet: The Fall of Fandana.*

Wreckless Planet is a trilogy, she says.

Of course, it is.

I hold it in my hands, turn it over and back. The binding is good and clean. The cover is matte, and the artwork is impressive. I flip through. A cursory glance. The font is Calibri, looks to be about 12 points, and the pages are cream. The book looks good.

Josie looks good.

A moment later we're inside, pulling, clutching, tripping, grabbing, undressing. She is exquisite, luscious, rich as candy – those hips, those thighs – and at this moment, she is mine.

We move to the couch, we move to the floor, we move to the mattress, up against the wall because there is no headboard, and I show her where the magic is made: not on the bed, or against the headboard, but wherever *I* happen to be, *me*, the king of this jungle, and she knows in that moment that I am both the alpha male and the omega man, the end all and be all, and soon her foolish bastard husband is going to know it, too.

I show her what I can do.

Josie gets loud.

Later, with her head on my chest, stroking her pretty copper hair, I marvel at how things can get carried away like that.

Her hair is in a tangle. I run my fingers through it. She smells divine.

Allan's book is on the floor when we come out of the bedroom. I pick it up, toss it on my desk. His picture is on the back cover. Black and white, like mine. Angled, like mine. Artsy, like mine.

But it isn't my wife adjusting her bra in *his* living room.

Josie leaves after another kiss, and I sit at my desk. I sit and I think. I can still smell her. I want her again, already.

After some time, I pick up his book and read, and I think of lions. Of lions, and dominance, and submission, and how lion cubs are born blind.

Allan's sentences are clunky. They are clunky and poorly structured, and rife with bad phrasing, bad usage. It's the work of a kid.

A fresher, younger male?

Allan is a blind cub.

He's no threat to me. Imitate all he wants, Allan is a toddler throwing the alphabet against the fridge. He may be loud, he may spread himself out, but there's no muscle behind the mane.

Why do we do this? Allan asks.

And I could tell him, right now, in this moment. I know why, holding his book in my hands and smelling his wife on my skin.

We do this to figure out why we do everything else. Why we suffer, why we work, why we resist, why we stop resisting.

We do *this* to understand *that*.

I could tell him in this moment.

But I won't.

He can read it here if he wants.

Poor bastard.

Part II
The Rights

Rights and Lefts

Two wrongs don't make a right
but three rights make a left
and three rights and a left
make a one-eighty
back the way we came
looking for the wrong turn
the missed exit
the way back
to where we were before.

It doesn't take a genius
to generalize this
human experience
mistakes were made
apologies issued
at the end of the day
and what was said
wasn't necessarily
what was meant
and what we meant to say
wasn't necessarily
what came out
when we opened our
mouths
and if we could take it all back
how many of us would?

Make three rights
and then a left
turn it around
and head the other way
hoping there's still enough

gas in the tank
and light in the sky
trying our best to get back
to where we were
but sometimes
when you get back
you find that
everyone you thought would be there
has gone somewhere else.

Three more rights
and another left
and we're right back
where we didn't think
we were supposed to be
thinking things over
and watching the time
and our lives
tick by
waiting for things
to line up
the way we thought
they were supposed to.

Three more rights and a left
three more rights
another left
and after that
we didn't even know
which way we were going
and by the end of it
the tank
was almost empty

and the sky
was almost dark
and most of those miles didn't matter
any damn way.

All Day Long

Woke up
fell down
got lost
a little while
paced a bit
picked up where I left off
then left off again.

She calls and calls and calls
and I'm thinking about
ditching the phone
getting a drone
and bombing her place
with notes that say
leave me alone.

She asked if I wanted
to grab some lunch
but I had the whole day set aside.

To do what?
To just think, I think.
All day long.

She doesn't get that
and she doesn't want to be alone
she doesn't *like* to be alone
and I try telling her
I don't always *like* to be alone
but sometimes I *need* to be alone
for an hour
a day

a week
a year
or maybe the rest of my life.

She calls and calls and calls
and when she reads this
I'm sure she'll start it up
all over again.

Go Tell Them

When you get down to it
there's no better way to start
than by burning down
everything that came before
and moving on
to the next plot
hammers, nails, and beams
handsaws
elbow grease
the last thing I'm afraid of
is a little hard work
idle hands
are the devil's playground
an idle self
is the American dream
I drive those nails
like I hate them
pound them down
until they won't go
no farther
double negatives
because I'm double angry
double salts
prime the explosives
wipe out everything
that came before
destroy build destroy
build
burn it down and start fresh
but most folks wouldn't dare
laziness
haziness

fear
craziness
(*genie-us?*)
when you get a second
go tell those folks
I'm a hardworking man
more so
than most.

Unforgiven

Forgive me
if I do not pick up
after myself
but I am only a man
(She says I have an excuse for everything
but I haven't come up with
an excuse for having so many excuses)
I was tired
it was a long week
and these pets
and the kids
and then there is myself
spilling coffee and not wiping it up
why?
I don't know
and if I had time to explain
I would've had time to wipe up the coffee
(There are things
I like to save
for a rainy day
such as housework
and everything else)
So forgive me
I am only a man alone with no guidance.
(Sacrificed
ran myself into the ground
and this is what I get in return. . .)

She says get your shit done
she says *real men* make time
for what's important

she says *boys*
have an excuse for everything
she says *I'm tired of your laziness*
(she didn't know that text
would work its way
into this poem)

I shrug it off.
I may be unforgiven
but at least I'm not ungrateful.

Again

Just when I thought
the dark days were over
one crept up on me
and now
I just want to sleep
forever and ever
amen
never hassle
with the ups and downs
the extraordinary transitions
from the far left to the far right
color spectrum
light bursting open
upon impact
prisms revealing
that all is not as it appears
I think I'll crawl back in bed
smother myself
with a pillow
and wait for the saving grace
of some random
stray
lost and confounded
bright beam
to shine upon my face.

Until then
here we go again.

Susie B. Sweet

All I ever wanted to be
was the boyfriend of Susie B. Sweet.

All I wanted
was to get that look,
you know,
from beyond the textbook.

From across the room,
that's it, right there,
that curt little smile,
that lingering stare,
and the note in pink
(big, loopy, and slow)
circle yes,
maybe,
or no.

Birthday Boy

I wish I could have gotten you
everything you wanted
everything you showed me
in the store
on the toy isle
plastic hopes and dreams
as I kissed the top of your head
saying, *Maybe for your birthday.*

I didn't know
that by the time your birthday came
I would be skipping meals
and saving the good food
for the days
when you and your brother stay
once again pawning my stuff
trying to keep the repo man
away from my truck
but I hide all that from you
shelter you
as best I can
and I scrounge up
enough money
to get you a few things
not everything you wanted
but just a few
just enough.

You're always happy
with what you get
and I'm always happy
when you are happy

and the three of us
are better off than most.

Even when we're broke.

Laundry

The laundry needs to be done
so the kids will have
clean clothes for school
(the older one stands behind me as I type
and asks
What are you writing?
I'm a loser I'm a loser I'm a loser?)

No, give me a minute, I say
and they laugh
and play
(for me it's coffee all day –
still barely enough
to escape the doldrums)
but I get the laundry started
so they'll have
clean clothes to wear
and miraculously
they do give me a minute
just long enough
to finish this poem.

The Frame

The fact is
the family was never good
at telling
the honest-to-God truth
(which truth?)
(this truth?)
never let the truth
get in the way
of a good story
or admit to yourself
when you're lying to yourself
just keep on keeping on
rose colored glasses
golden frames
golden fibs
painted
like oil on canvas.

(have these stories taken root,
my son?
have they grown leaves
and risen on giant stalks
in your heart
my young son?)

It's not a lie
if it's true
and it's not true
if it's a lie
but there's a space
just between the truth and the lie
a border

a frame
between the painting and the wall.

(Follow me
into the dark
where life can be
anything we want
even when it's not)

The crowd arrives with the rising sun
and there the boy sits
a golden frame
around a golden fib
a canvas
slashed angrily
with golden hues
and the crowd marvels.

(The stories have taken root
and risen on giant stalks
too big, now,
to cut down
so just look at the painting
and move on.)

Promise

I will work harder
I will work harder
because I want this more
I want this life
more
than you do
and I live it
I claim it
as my own
from the moment I rise
to the moment I die
I live for this
I need this
like eating
sleeping
breathing
blinking
this is *mine*
and I claim it as my own
the odds and ins
ups and downs
nouns and pronouns
this life
I was created for
bred into
raised on stories and keyboard clacks
stitched together
heart and soul
by a thread of discontent
and a hundred-thousand needle jabs
this life of mine
this life

this craft
I claim it as my own
because I was made for this
every loop and tug of the thread
pulling the seams tighter
made for this
bred for this
put together
like casebound binding
for this
and I want this
I want this
I *need* this
more than you do
I
promise
you
that.

Ghetto Dwelling

The apartments
are run down
sitting on the edge of town
with nothing behind them
but empty fields
and the people there
spend their days
watching tv
and complaining
waiting for assistance
waiting for checks
waiting for handouts
and bailouts
and whatever happens to them next
and I'm beginning to think
this
is
part
of the
problem.

Giving It a Go

Cleared a spot against the wall
assembled the bed frame
put on the box spring and mattress
sheets blankets pillow
now maybe I'll get some sleep.

Been sleeping on the couch
or the floor,
for a good, long while.

Haven't had a cigarette in months.

Eat better
exercise
try to lessen the stress in your life.

Salads
and lean-meat sandwiches.

Cutting back on everything
and trying to cut up a little more
but somewhere along the way
I'm afraid
I lost my sense of humor
maybe while I was sleeping
on the couch
I think I should pull up the cushions
check things out
see if that's where it's been
these last few months.

I don't know why

assembling a bed
should feel like giving in
or giving up
but it does
as if sleeping on the couch
had anything to do
with anything
I'm trying to prove
or maybe it's just a thing
you get used to
like being alone,
eating bad food,
smoking,
and wasting time.

Re-entry

We didn't know if we were going to
burn up, blow up,
or what!
The whole damn shuttle started shaking. . .

I waited for her
just inside the doors.
The girl at the front tried to talk to me
but everything I said was gibberish
and I couldn't stop checking my phone.

It's a heat,
a hellish heat like you wouldn't believe
and the only thing between you and that heat
are the tiles,
if not for the tiles
the whole thing would burn right up.

She texted that she'd missed her exit.
I waited.
There isn't much that makes me nervous,
anymore,
but I was nervous.

I like being on stage,
or behind the table,
signing books.

Those things are easy,
easier to do
than standing up
and opening the door for a pretty girl

or waiting on one who missed her exit.

The whole damn thing started shaking
so bad I thought for sure
this was the end of us.
I could imagine those tiles coming off
one after the other
and then after that, you know. . .

She made it
and I stood up and opened the door for her.
I felt shaky
but I hid it well.
When we talked about it later,
laughed about it,
she said she couldn't tell I was nervous.

I could tell she was,
and that made things easier.

I had been by myself a good long while,
floating in outer space,
drifting in orbit,
with nothing to pin me down.

No surprise, then,
that I was shaking.

That's just a part of re-entry.

On the Cushy Blue Couch

She was talking
the first time I kissed her.
We were sitting
in her living room
on the cushy blue couch
and she was talking.

I meant to go home.
We had met earlier for coffee
and I'd gone to do some work
and the whole time
I wished I had kissed her.

She was talking
but after awhile
I have to admit
I wasn't listening
not because I didn't want to
but because I couldn't
think
focus
concentrate
on anything but her mouth.

I pulled her close
and we kissed
there on the cushy blue couch.

That's one way to shut me up
she said
after.

I held her awhile
after that
and neither of us said anything
and everything was right with the world.

Months later
she gave the couch away
when she moved into my place.

I'm glad she kept the kiss.

The Best of Days

When the wind dies down
I tell her
we're going to go outside
hold hands
in the sun
sit in chairs
and talk about all the things we haven't done.

When the rain stops
I say
We'll take a walk
while everything is still wet
clean and fresh
newborn and alive.

When the clouds move on
I say
we won't ever think about them again
about this dark time
and the dark times to come.

I'll keep the curtain pulled back
I say
so I can see outside
so I'll know
when the storm has passed
because otherwise I might miss
the best of days.

Ballgame

He knows he can hit
during practice
but the game
is a whole 'nother thing
and after two strike-outs
he's feeling unsure
so I go to him
at the dug out
and put my hand against the chain link
and tell him to look for me
when he's at the plate
I tell him
to look for me
and when he sees where I'm standing
to point his feet in my direction
and to cock his bat all the way back
and he nods
and I nod
and our hands touch through the fence.

He doesn't understand
conservation of motion
but he understands
I'm there to help
and in a little while
he's at the plate again
and I pick my spot
and he looks for me through the face mask
and sees me
and I motion for his feet
and having seen where I stand

he aligns his feet
and brings the bat up
and the pitch is thrown
he swings
there is the sound of contact
and he runs.

I love him and he knows it
and I know time is a thief
and I won't always be there
but if I've done my job right
he'll at least have a notion
of where I would be standing
when he doesn't know what to do
and I hope
if I've done my job right
he'll trust
and have faith
when those moments come.

I don't always know what to do
but I do my best
to stand
in the right place.

I love him too much
to stand anywhere else.

A Nice Lunch

She has enticing eyes
and a good smile
great body
hips and all
and I'm thinking about her
more than I should.

(I saw a boy
carrying a project
on the sidewalk at school
so worried about what this girl was doing
that he dropped it
and it broke all to pieces)

Keep your eye on the ball
keep the ball in your court
keep your court clean
and free of debris
and remember which goal
you're running towards.

We had a nice lunch
at an expensive place
and she told me about her
kids
family
friends
and ambitions.

We split dessert
and I couldn't complain.

(I saw a man
driving through the neighborhood
lost
driving back and forth
lost
up one street and down the other
lost
until he ran out of gas)

I'm thinking about her
too much today
with the rain falling
thunder and lightning
old typewriter
typing
wondering what she's doing
and wishing she would just
go away
so I could quit thinking about her.

(I once saw a man
miss his flight
because he was standing
at the window
by himself
watching planes take off
into the sky)

There could be more to the story:
happiness
love
a whole-life
rather than this half-life

lived by myself
but I don't know,
I don't know,
I don't know.

(I once saw a man
giving away
everything he owned
and when I asked why
he said
he was afraid
he might lose it)

I won't call her again.

She'll think it was because
she did something wrong.

She won't know it was because
she did everything right.

Lightning Bugs

For a long time
I went around with notebooks
catching moments
like lightning bugs
jarring them up
on the page
lining them up
on the shelf
so I could watch them all glow.

There were never
too many to catch before.

Before
there were only a few,
big, fat, slow,
lazy and angry
easy to grab
and jar up.

I thought I'd seen them all
(the important ones, at least)
until I met her.

She took my hand
and moments flew up
out of nowhere
thousands
too many to catch
and so a great many of them
got away.

I wish I could have
captured them all
but I don't mind.

At least I got to see them glowing
as they went.

Thief

A thief came
and took
the leaves from the trees
and then
painted the sky gray
and then
killed the
grass
weeds
flowers
and then
as if that wasn't enough
stole all the warmth
from this old house
and then
started sticking sticky fingers
into every little thought
in my head
every thought that things might be
okay
and then
just when he thought
he had taken
everything
I surprised him
by writing this.

Scars

Nobody makes it
as long as we have
without a few scars.

She has a few
and I have a few
and maybe that's why
things work
between us.

Mowed her yard
as a surprise
and she brought dinner.
I hadn't seen her
for three days
and was astounded
all over again
at how pretty she is.

After the yard was mowed
we ate in the living room
on the sofa
and I felt
right
at
home.

We talked about our scars
how she got hers
how I got mine
and the lessons learned.

Some of mine are ugly
and they run deep
but she didn't shy away
when I showed her.

She still hasn't.

Before Her

Before
there was no coffee creamer
in the fridge
and the laundry was never folded.

Before
there was no laundry basket
on the bathroom floor.

No
fridge
kitchen table
reasonable dinner.

I did without a lot
of the usual comforts
and in a way
prided myself on that.

(I am
not one of you
and I
do not need
comfort
warmth
affection
peace
or love)

Before
there were a great many things
I did without

and I could do without
those things again.

As long as I still have her.

Lunch

Not the first time
I came to your school
to surprise you
eat lunch with you
but that day
in September
was a little different.

I try to shelter you
from the worst of it
but it gets pretty bad sometimes
so I hide it here
for all the world to see
(go figure)
but that day in September
I showed up
with some *Taco Bell*
and waited for your class
I wore the Superman shirt
big mistake at an elementary school
because then I had to show off
some superpowers
to prove that
yes
I am the real Superman.

The kids were excited
but I was waiting for you
and when we saw each other
we both smiled
and we hugged

because in second grade
you aren't too big
to hug your dad
and we went into the cafeteria
and sat at our own table
and ate
and talked.

I made you laugh
and you made me see
why I do what I do
trying my best
to keep my head together
and what you didn't know
was that I left my phone in the truck
to keep the bill collectors
from interrupting our lunch
and what you didn't know
was yet again
everything was falling apart
and yet again
Superman
was mustering all his strength
to fly around the world backwards
to stop time
for just a bit
just long enough
for the two of us
to laugh
and talk
and eat
and what you didn't know
was that day in September

was rock-bottom-bad
but that half-hour in the lunchroom
sitting with you
at our own little table
was the best.

Warmth

She
is like the sun
shining after many winter days
radiant, warm, beautiful,
like spring
after many winter days
alive and lovely
soft, sweet, elegant,
a place you want to be
like home
after many days away
and her hands have done more
for my soul
in one day
than all the
many winter days
of typing, writing,
book signing,
singing,
and guitar slinging
could have ever done.

She is like something
you didn't know you needed
until you found it
like something
you didn't know was missing
until you stumbled upon it
and then wondered
how you ever did without.

After many winter days

it is a relief
to live
in her warm
embrace.

Like Pieces of the Same Puzzle

She's been through a lot
I won't tell you what
because that's her business
but I'll tell you
that neither of us
has had it easy
in this world

(When I hold you
all of that
falls away
and I know
I have finally
arrived)

Before there can be a show
there has to be
a rehearsal
a setup
a sound check
and every *happily ever after*
begins with
once upon a time.

(The rest of this
world
this
life
loses its sting
when I'm with you
when I'm with you
I live)

Every pay off begins with a build-up
setting the scene
anticipation
and tension.

Hunger
sweetens
the feast.

(We fit together
like pieces
of the same puzzle
like
harmonies
like
yellow and blue
make
green)

We've been through a lot
each of us
in our own way
in our own time
our own
private
pain.

These things prepared us
for each other.

Dynamite Mornings

We shake the kids awake
with earthquakes
and dynamite
and still they
slowly
open
their
eyes
blinking
and rubbing them
before falling back into their pillows
fast
asleep
and dreaming
that it's
time
to
wake
up.

Prophesying

We go around
speaking the future
into our own lives
prophesying
our own
success
or failure
conjuring
daily
tomorrow's
weather.

The Big Check

Scrounged up enough change
to make the drive
to get the kids
the day before the big check
came through.

It was a Thursday
and we were thirsty
but we had to wait and see.

The collectors call
and call and call
until you want to
kill
them
all.

The kids brought their stuff
in backpacks
full of knickknacks
games
movies for us to watch together.

We made burgers
we made fries
we made a good time
out of nothing at all
laughing and joking
and cracking up
like we had money in the bank.

Call after call

message after message.

I put the phone on silent
and changed my inbox settings
from English to Spanish
just to throw them a little.

The kids made me laugh
and the collectors made me hate
everything but the kids.
We decided to play *bill collector*
and the kids shook me down
for every dime I had left.

They pretended to call
and I pretended to not answer.

I decided
that however resolved the collectors were
to collecting
I was more resolved
to not paying.

You know,
on principle.

We played our games
and watched our movies.

Money or no money
we had fun
and the next day
when the big check came through

we went grocery shopping.

The collectors got
not one penny.

Catapult

We built a catapult for flinging bad people out of town. This was after society collapsed, although I'd say we were pretty civilized while we were building the catapult. It was a team effort.

We had an architect on hand. He used to be an architect before society collapsed, and he drew up the plans: He, and this other guy who used to be a physicist. They worked out the plans together one day, sitting at a picnic table at the park. Some women brought them bread and fish, and they worked out the dimensions, the materials, stress loads, all that stuff. All the forces required to fling a bad person out of town.

We had several guys in town who used to be in construction. They were essential, and the work was good. We all agreed it was good to be doing something, seeing as how we had been doing much of nothing since society collapsed. Nothing but spinning our wheels talking about why society had collapsed, how it had collapsed, how it could be rebuilt, and whether or not it would collapse again if it were.

So we built the catapult, and we were all happy with ourselves.

There had been a big end-of-the-world party following the collapse when it became apparent our frozen food would rot if we didn't eat it. We ate for two days straight, and we all got sick, and then we all slept for another day or so.

Everyone looked to the mayor for guidance when the grid went down and the trucks stopped showing up at the supermarket. The mayor had no good answers, and there was talk of electing a new mayor, but there were few good candidates. Some folks felt this was our

SJ Duncan

chance to rebuild society in ways vastly different from anything we'd ever known. We would usher in a new dawn for mankind, a new era of equality, and peace, and prosperity. There would be hope, and love, and equal distribution of goods and wealth, and so on, and so forth.

All that socialist talk made for a night of good sleep, but the next morning, when half the town got the notion that equality meant they could do zero work and still get pancakes, the rest of us made it clear that equality meant *equal opportunity*, not *equal pancakes*.

There was talk of roving bandits, biker gangs, outlaws, and renegade soldiers armed with heavy artillery, and so we assigned men to watch the roads in and out of town. There was an incident one day, and a man got shot trying to get through. He was headed north, looking for his people, and there was no good reason to shoot him. There was talk of flinging the guy who'd shot the traveler, but the catapult wasn't ready at that time. The guy who shot the other guy claimed it was a tragic misunderstanding, and cited precedence set by other great misunderstandings which had occurred since the collapse of society. He used to be a lawyer. We didn't fling him out of town, even after the catapult was finished.

There was talk of sending letters to neighboring towns to see how they were dealing with society collapsing. We nominated our local mailman, but he reminded us that society had collapsed, and informed us that he was no longer a mailman and that we could deliver our own effing letters. He was then nominated to be flung out of town, but the lawyer cited the precedence of other people who had been one thing before society collapsed, and who now considered themselves to be something else, such as Jerry McFinten, our local journalist, who now whittled knickknacks for the kids. We didn't fling the mailman. And anyhow, argued the lawyer, the post office guaranteed mail delivery through rain, sleet, snow, hail, and gloom of night, but made no promises regarding the collapse of society.

There was talk of getting the local economy moving again. There was talk of how to pay for the catapult. There was talk of flinging anyone who talked of how to pay for the catapult out of town. The catapult was paid for, anyhow. The materials were donated, and the labor was free.

One day we all realized we'd lost track of the days. The librarian believed it to be Monday, but she wasn't sure. The clerk from city hall swore it was Tuesday, but the pastor from the First Baptist church agreed with the librarian, and pretty soon everyone who thought it was Monday wanted to fling those who thought it was Tuesday, and vice versa. We nominated a man to be the official keeper of days and told him to start with Wednesday.

Nobody was happy.

We decided to put ourselves back to work. The people who hated the work wanted six-hour work days. The people who liked the work wanted twelve-hour days, just to stay occupied. We agreed on nine-hour days. A guy named Lawson, who had wanted six-hour days, lost his mind and started threatening the mayor with a brick. Lawson was subdued, and we cranked the catapult back, but Lawson came to his senses.

We did not fling him out of town.

On a different day a man named Gary Geysner lost *his* mind, and stripped naked, and went up and down Main Street screaming about bigfoot, and aliens, and the Illuminati, and what-have-you. He was subdued and made to wear a pair of briefs and was put on the catapult. The catapult was still cranked back from when Lawson was on it, but this time we came within two hairs of flinging Gary Geysner, but Gary came to his senses, and begged for mercy, and was not flung out of town.

It seemed we were all getting a little fragile. It also seemed that each time there was an incident, we got closer and closer to actually flinging somebody out of town. There was a moment when we all took a good, hard look at ourselves, realized what monsters we had become, and began dismantling our catapult.

Then, a week later, we heard that the town across the river had built *themselves* a catapult.

So we built two.

So they built another.

So we built another, just to keep ahead.

In the midst of all this catapult building, however, we realized we were no longer thinking of ourselves as a collapsed society: We were a society again. A society that builds catapults to aim at other societies.

We have yet to fling a bad person out of town.

Right now, we have more catapults than any town within striking distance.

As a society, we have decided that we can live with that.

We've also decided it wouldn't hurt to build a few more.

Just in case.

Part III
The Left

Lion

I am a lion.
I know this
because I heard myself roar
the other day
in the morning
when no one was around.

Scared myself a little
at first
but once you've done it the first time
you want to try it again.

You want them to know
that you know
that you are a lion.

On occasion
you may claw the walls
and shed on the bed
but that's expected.

Be the king
of your habitat
and lord help you
if it goes to your head.

Shake out your mane
and be the man,
lion.

Day Job

Mikey hates the day job
but he keeps it
because it feeds the kids.

Julie drives a good car
the day job bought
and together
at night
they watch TV
the day job pays for.

They are young
and I wish I could tell them what I know
about being young
and about day jobs
and about losing your mind
slowly
one day at a time
but one thing I know about being young
is that young people don't listen.

The day job
got them a new fridge
when the old one went out
a few weeks ago.
I helped Mikey
get it up the steps
wishing all the while
that I could tell him what I know
about young people
and their refrigerators
but if there's one thing I know

about young people
it's that they don't listen
and they don't clean their refrigerators
often enough.

The day job pays
for all those diapers they go through
diaper after diaper
and now there's another baby on the way.

The day job is going to pay for that, too.

Mikey plays guitar
on the porch
and I listen
from my porch
and sometimes I ask him
how his music is coming along
and he always says, "Couldn't be better."

The day job paid for the guitar
and the porch.

The guitar hasn't paid
for anything.

I'm nosey
and probably bossy, too,
but I leave them alone,
Mikey and Julie.
I leave them to be young
and work day jobs
that pay for diapers

and food
and houses and cars and guitars.

Mikey comes home cussing
about the day job
some days
and I nod to myself
knowing what I know about
young people
and cussing
and day jobs.

Every generation thinks
they are the first to discover
love
sex
death
rock n' roll
poetry
politics
and the need
to make money to buy things
which requires a person
to take up a day job.

Young people
think they know everything.

Then they lose their minds
slowly
day after day
at their day jobs
and by the time they figure it all out

they are old people
surrounded by young people
who don't listen.

I pity them
more than I envy them.

Mikey lost the day job
but Julie found one
and so Mikey started staying home
with the babies
and Julie would come home
cussing about the day job.

Mikey hardly ever plays guitar
on the front porch
anymore.

After awhile
Mikey got another day job
but Julie kept her day job
and so there were two day jobs
paying for things
and the kids went to day care
and Mikey and Julie got put on opposite
shifts
and now they never see each other.

I see them both
leaving and coming home
at opposite ends of the day.

I think they're both

having affairs.

I wish I could sit them down
both of them
and tell them what I know about
affairs
and marriage
and day jobs
and babies
and coming home cussing
and never playing guitar
on the porch anymore
and losing your mind
an
hour
at
a
time
and all the rest
but I don't
because they're young
and young people don't listen.

I know I didn't.

Flying Kites

In so many ways
I'm still there
and I'm still him
that sixteen-year-old kid
out of control
out of line
and locked away
out of sight.

Twenty years have gone by
twenty years
and I'm doing alright
I've got this writing thing going
and most days I know who
and where
I am
but every now and then
I think of that little cell
on the fifth floor
of the county courthouse
and all the time I spent in it.

They don't use that place anymore.
These days the bad kids
the out-of-control kids
the delinquents
go in a building just down the road
and I don't know if it's nicer or cleaner
or if the kids ever get to
come out of their cells
but I know that in many ways
it's probably exactly the same

kids writing letters
to the outside world
and trying not to lose their minds.

In so many ways
I'm still there
and I'm still him
and I'm still writing letters
and trying not to lose my mind.

I still send my scribblings
out into the free world.

People pay
to read them
now.

Better Late Than Early

Running late
again
but still I sit
at this machine
just a moment longer
hoping to catch
the right words
or some good ones
at least
watching the clock
knowing I need to go
but the catch is
I need this
more than I need
to be on time
so if you don't mind
waiting
just a few more minutes
I'm almost done
with this poem.

Keys, phone, wallet,
I'm on my way.

Paper in the Chamber

I keep paper in the drawer
and one in the chamber
locked and loaded
ready to pop off
at a moment's notice
because moments don't usually
make themselves known
before hand
but I'm steady
with my clean sheet
rolled and ready
behind the ribbon
and when the moment comes I
poppoppoppop
good times
bad times
my time
is spent working on this
doing what I need to do
daily
until
I'm
dismissed.

Spectrum

It's hard to pin-point
the moment of change
from worm to moth
from caterpillar to butterfly.

Transitions
the place
between fact
and superstition
the line
between hitting
and missing.

After some time has passed
you look back
at everything you've been through
and marvel –
I'm not the same person anymore.

Your friends don't get that
sometimes.
Sometimes they don't get
that the person they loved is gone.

Did he die?

No.

He grew wings.
Now he can fly.

They still see

some of the old colors
in your spectrum
blue where they expect blue
but then sometimes they see yellow
where they expect red
and can't understand
why.

I'm sorry to say
my friend
that the cocoon has been torn
and left behind –
from darkness
to bright blue sky.

Sometimes
they have trouble understanding
and then sometimes
you look at them
and realize they have shifted
too.

Sometimes you realize
there is now an entire spectrum
between the two of you.

Sometimes you feel bad for them
those old friends
digging with sticks
at your empty cocoon.

Crossing i's

He writes about you
in the dark
where you can't read it.

He writes about the things
that hurt the most
pencil scribbling
in the dark
making ghost whispers
a thousand
little
hurts
whispering in the dark
I was a child,
it's not my fault.

(Every time you dot an i
a devil chokes and dies)

I wish he didn't have to do this
but these are the things
he can't say
because they would hurt you
but he can't keep to himself
because they hurt him
and so he crosses his t's
and dots his i's
and hopes you never know why.

Forgiveness,
says the good book.

Forgiveness, says the man I've become.

(what the mute need to say
the deaf need to hear)

I have forgiven you
me
the man I am today
has forgiven you
for all the little hurts
along the way
but the boy won't forget
that boy
with the shaggy brown hair
sitting on the floor
writing with the lights off
so you can't sneak in and read it.

Ghost scribbles
crossing t's
(*Lord, help me please*)
and dotting i's
(*another devil dies*).

(what the mute need to say
the deaf need to hear)

He doesn't listen
that boy
and no one ever speaks.

I told him it was okay
the man I've become

tries to tell him
that he was good enough
good enough
good enough
but sometimes I'm afraid
the boy
has gone deaf.

(what the mute need to say
the deaf need to hear)

He just
scribbles away
a thousand little hurts
day after day
page after page
dotting i's
until all the devils die.

(there is always another devil –
always.)

So he writes about you in the dark
where you can't read it
and he says the things he needs to say
and I'm afraid
he's shattered the light bulb in there
so even if we try the switch
nothing
will ever
change.

(condemned to sit

like a rat in a cage
scribbling
ever more
in
rage)

I love the boy, now.

I wish he could
love himself
but the boy
doesn't know how.

Little Cousin

Things were the same
at the cemetery
the same as they had been on that day
twelve years before
when we buried him.

(Little cousin,
why did you have to go so soon?
We were having so much fun.)

I hadn't been in awhile
but I got the notion to go
and so I went.

There's a bench by his grave
and I sat
and what I thought I wanted to say
escaped me
and what I said instead was,
I haven't forgotten you
I haven't forgotten you...

I don't know if it's proper
to ask the dead for favors
but sometimes I do
sometimes I ask him
in case he can sway things
one way or another
or knows somebody who can.

Sitting by his grave
it occurs to me

that I have the rest of my life to live
and there will be other graves to sit by.

This hits me all at once.

I will lose more people
and they will lose me.

I talk to him,
tell him I'm doing good,
tell him I'm trying my best,
trying to do right
even when I don't know which way to turn.
I talk to him
and tell him I miss him
and tell him I haven't forgotten him
and after a while I get up to go.

I almost leave
and then I turn around
and ask him a favor.

On the way out
I think about old times
the two of us
playing in the woods
making up games
and writing stories.

He was eighteen when he died
on I-20.

In a few years

he will have been in the ground
as long as he was above it
and then longer.

In the end
we all spend more time
in it
than on it.

Somehow
that makes me feel
just a little better
about asking favors.

Like Art

It feels good
being
where you are supposed to be
and doing
what you are supposed to do
and knowing
you have finally found your way
found it or made it
like art
painted
like art
created
like shapes
blasted out of a mountain side.

It feels good
after being so human for so long.

It feels good being
on display.

Supersets

You do your squats first.
You do them
and after
without resting
you get in a plank position
and you hold.

The stopwatch counts.

Back to back,
back to back,
one exercise
followed by another
without rest.

Supersets.

Planks strengthen your core.
We all know about squats.
Nobody wants to hear about squats.

The stopwatch counts.
Your core trembles, burns.
One of the cats climbs up your body
all claws
and you curse
but you hold your position.

There is a reason
you do the things you do.

Goals to achieve.

The stopwatch counts.
The cat darts away.

Tomorrow you'll get up early
write
do a book signing
and then play a show without resting.

Supersets.

Erasers

We spend too much time
losing pieces of ourselves
on old mistakes
like pencil erasers
rubbing and rubbing and rubbing. . .

No one makes it
without regrets
so take it easy on yourself,
youngster.
We're all learning to write
and no one learns to write
without misspelling a few words.

Don't worry about it
and don't rub yourself raw
over something
that doesn't matter anyway.

A misspelled word here and there
doesn't mean
the piece is ruined.
It means
you're human.

Lucky

The old truck
wouldn't start.

It was hot
in the parking lot
and we knew it was the starter
because the starter had been going out
for some time
but this time
no amount of banging on it
would turn it over.

These things happen
more often to some
than others.

It was payday
and there was money in the bank –
money that would be gone
the next day.

Bills, bills, bills.

We walked down to the parts store
and got a new starter
and changed it out
in the parking lot
in the heat of midday
with sweat running down our faces
like we were melting.

We got the truck running again.

Hot and wet
and grimy from crawling under the truck
we went to get a bite to eat.

Sometimes bad things happen on payday.

Sometimes you get lucky like that.

Good Days

These are good days
Spring break
with my boys
playing
like I'm a kid again
and feeling better than I have
in a good long while
hitting the weight bench
working out
bouncing back
getting all up in the world's face
a middle finger free-for-all
even after a good, hard fall
the ego is still through the roof
and you can't tell me what to do.

Maybe I'm doing good work
and maybe I'm not
but the point is I'm working
moving
shucking and jiving
and riding my own lightning
once again.

Remember those little lines?

The ones we write
without caring who reads them?

Yeah.

These are some of those.

Slosh

We pour our hearts out
daily
in one way or another
spilling parts of ourselves
as we walk
our hearts sloshing around
like open buckets of paint
spilling here and there
on the carpet
the couch
on our nice
new shoes.

We pour them out
and mostly what we want
is for someone to notice the colors
the shades
we point to the mess we've made
and say
look, see there, right there,
but few stop to see
and most want to paint over
our splashes.

But we continue on
day by day
spilling ourselves
as we walk
leaving trails
beautiful trails
ugly trails
muddied trails

on the path behind
and sometimes
on
each other.

Waiting in Cars at Lights

They sit in their cars
at the traffic light
each of them
alone in their cars
not looking at each other
not talking to each other
listening to their radios
looking at their phones
sitting alone in their cars
sitting still
waiting on things to change.

Gauging by the Lines

We sat on the floor
in the bathroom
watching the sunlight crawl
across the tile.

You can see it moving,
the sunlight,
if you gauge it by the lines in the tile.
A minute
two minutes
not long at all
and you can see how far the light has crept
and you begin to feel
the whole day slipping away.

She had been cleaning the tub
and I was talking
not helping
like I should have been
just talking
and watching the sunlight.

The bathroom
smelled like Pine-Sol
and the light was vivid
bright
pouring through the open window.

She didn't see it at first
the movement
but after a while she could, too,
and then we were both on the floor watching it.

The light crept steadily
from one line
to the next
slow enough so you didn't notice it
but fast enough to see
if you watched closely.

I began thinking our lives are like that:
Slow enough
so you don't notice your days slipping away
but fast enough to see
if you care to.

You don't want to waste the time
given to you
but then again
wasting time can lead to
some interesting insights.

In all
I feel like our time
was well spent that day
on the floor
in the bathroom
watching the sunlight
creep across the tile.

Reins

Enjoying the here and now
but I can't wait to see the path
my life takes
the ups and downs
the peak
the decline
like a VH1
behind the music
back-story
suppository
and on and on.

Better than the best
and the baddest
by far.

For now
I have my hands on the reigns
I have control of this thing
I have it in my grasp
and I don't know which of us
leads the other
but I'm not worried about
where we're going.

I can see something
at the end of the path
and something
is better than nothing,
which is all I could see before.

Shooting Plastic Ducks

The ducks at the fair
are yellow and plastic
with red bulls-eyes painted on them
and they move on a chain-belt
so swiftly
it's tricky to get your shot in.

We plink, and plink,
and plink away at them
but there's always another duck
coming fast
right on the tail
of the one before.

Standing there
as the ducks go by
I look to the kids
all laughing and smiling and plinking.

There is so much
I want to tell them
about life
love
success
failure
how to age
how to be happy
how to be fair
but there are
always more
things to say
than hours in the day

or opportunities
because the best things
the most important things
can't be said
just any ol' time.

You have to wait
to say those things.

You have to wait
until you see the bulls-eye.

Daily
I think of something to tell them
something else
I want them to know
that might serve them
somehow
someday
but sometimes the day gets in the way
of telling them everything.

Plinking
the kids laugh
and I think of all the things
I may never get a chance to say
because time and opportunity whiz by
so quickly
and you can only line up
so many good shots
so I say what I need to say
when I can
and take my shots

when I see the bulls-eye
and by the time
they are grown
I hope
I've hit enough ducks
to win everyone a prize.

This Guy, Here and Now

I wanted to be that guy
at one time
that writer
in that city
writing about
those people
in that place
at that time
but life
or circumstance
or God
didn't put me there
then
with them
as him.

I wanted to be
that guy
at one time
but somewhere along the way
in pursuit of that guy
I became this one
which is fine with me.

I like this guy better
anyhow.

Missed Opportunity

I didn't capture the room
when I wrote all those poems
that became the book
that set me on this path
and for which I am thankful.

They were all I could manage to write
at the time
living in the backroom
of my sister's house
counting change
just to buy food and gas
and trying to keep my head together.

I always worked
and provided for my kids
and I was finally able to write my way
out of my own prison
but I didn't capture the room
with the two windows
the piecemeal carpet
the cracks in the walls
the air-up mattress with a single sheet
stacks of books
a few guitars
and that desk.

I didn't capture the room
when I wrote that first book
I guess because
I was trying
to escape it.

Dirt Bike

You are going to get kicked
stepped on
and ignored
and you'll want to give up.

It happens to all of us
and there's no way around it.

The strong survive
the strong and smart thrive
and the ones who can be honest
with themselves
have an easier time
adapting.

If I mess up
I want to know it
so I can fix it.

Don't coddle me:
Throttle me.

And watch me
take off
like a
dirt bike.

These Little Things

When you look down
and realize
there are enough of
these little things
for another book
another
(What has this been,
not *The Long Dark Lonesome*,
but maybe
The Short Bright Daydream?)
you think to yourself
maybe it's going to be alright
after all
after Fall
and Winter
have come and gone
after all those cold days
have dragged on and on
and then everything explodes
life
love
personal growth
you think
we've survived another blow
another course
on the way to our master's
in feeling low
and yet still
we're the first body
to dance around the maypole
maybe we have this thing
at least

under control
and who knows
now that we have enough
of these little things
for another go
who knows
what might happen next.

Neighborhood

There are nine houses
in the neighborhood
and a lot of trees
between the first five
and the last four
and it's quiet
usually
when the big black dog
isn't barking.

The road is asphalt
single lane
and when you pass one another
you each have to
drive in the ditch
but that's how it is
with everything
I think.

We mow on Saturdays
usually the older couple starts it
and the rest of us follow suit
so we don't look like
lazy white trash
and I've never seen
the older couple
smile at anyone
I think
because they wish
we weren't here.

We have kids

and the people beside us
have kids
and somebody down the street
has kids
but the kids are all good
and nothing gets vandalized.

Across the street from our house
is a fenced area
with two deer
and a few goats.
I can see them through the window
when I'm writing.

We're looking to buy land
with a lot of trees
and when we do
we'll leave this neighborhood behind
and somebody else
will watch the deer
and the goats
through the window
or maybe
they'll just watch tv.

I wonder if they'll mow
when the old couple mows
or if they'll let the yard
get out of control.

The realtor suggests
this plot of land
or that one

ten acres here
twenty-five there
on a private road.

Trees,
I tell her.
Lots and lots of trees
and no neighbors.

While she looks for land
with lots and lots of trees
and no neighbors
we go about our business
mowing when the old couple mows
and driving in the ditch
to pass one another
on the single lane asphalt.

Someday
we'll sit on a porch
surrounded by trees
and it won't matter
if the grass
gets a little tall.

This Writing Thing

You wonder sometimes
how this all got started
this writing thing
this sitting-alone-for-hours thing
this spilling-your-heart-to-the-world thing
you remember that old typewriter
and sitting down with it
after school
elementary school
writing flip-books for your friends
attention, attention
everyone
may I have your attention
because I'm not getting it
any other way
flip-books for friends
stapled in the crease
and stories about werewolves
and vampires
it was never about money
it was about
I like your story
you're a good writer
write another one, Steven,
write a scary one
write a funny one
write one about the school
and so you write
you write
because nothing
can touch you
when you're writing

you're invincible
and powerful
sitting at that typewriter
you're above it all
out of reach
superhuman and safe
safe
it was a safe place to be
where no one
pushed you around
and it didn't matter if you
made a mistake
or if it wasn't good enough
you had time
to fix the mistakes
before anyone saw
what you'd made
it was a safe place to be
and maybe that's how it got
out of hand
because when you feel unsafe
and you find a safe place
you want to stay there
forever.

One Bite at a Time

The road rolls out
like ribbons and streamers
out west and back
down south and back
north
and east
any which way
you want to go.

Suitcases and directions
itineraries
maps
sunglasses
snacks
sunshine
roadside attractions
stop
and post a selfie.

The suitcase is in the back
with the laptop
up early at the hotel
complimentary breakfast
and coffee
getting some writing done
and living the dream.

The road rolls out
like a ribbon
like a streamer
blow the horn
this is your party

the one you put on for yourself
and even if no one shows up
we're having cake
cookies
and ice cream
(you scream, the cheering fans scream)
taking bites out of the world
one bite at a time
trying to eat it up
before it eats you.

The road rolls out like a streamer
over hills and into valleys
blow the horn
this is the life
radio up
windows down
working your way
through the world
grabbing at the cake
like a kid
who never learned
to keep his hands to himself.

Set up and sit
behind the table
and sign your name
sign your name
sign your name. . .

Head back home
a different route
following the streamers

and trying to eat up
as much of the world as you can
living
living
and loving it
happy birthday, baby,
every day is your day
because you've made it that way
grabbing at the cake
grabbing at the cake
and maybe
just maybe
you can get a big bite
before somebody slaps your hand.

Working

Wake up at 5 AM
start the coffee
and get a jump
on the day.

Do it for the fans
do it for your friends
but mostly you just do it
for yourself.

Give the impression
that you live a life of leisure
a life
people
admire and envy.

There are phone calls to make
artwork to approve
questions to answer
words to choose.

The devil's in the details
so you spend your days
with the devil
sweating the small stuff.

They want pictures with you
even when your hair
is not
cooperating.

Trade the 9 to 5

for a 24/7
and maybe you start making
good money
but if you factor in
all those years you worked for free
for the love of the thing
the numbers don't add up.

They look at you
sometimes
like you're not one of them.

Don't bother explaining
that you are.

They won't believe you anyway.

All it takes
is more work
patience
and persistence
than most people
are willing to put in.

Go ahead
and tell them
that you are just like them
as you sign the book
and smile for the camera.

Then get up
at five the next morning
start the coffee

and get a jump
on another day.

Morning Cups

The hotel room smelled like shampoo, steam, and heat. Tara had opened the bathroom door to defog the mirror while she dried her hair. After a few minutes, the whirring of the hairdryer stopped, and Tara asked if there was any coffee. I told her we drank it all the evening before.

"I won't make it far without my morning cup," she said.

I agreed I wouldn't, either.

Then, without our morning cups, we managed to gather our stuff and check out.

The lobby was also out of coffee, but there was an *Alon* next door and we needed gas, so we stopped there. Tara went inside as I filled the tank. I couldn't wait to have my morning cup. I felt slow and sluggish. Lazy. And we had a full day of driving ahead. Midland had been good to us and this book signing had been the best by far. I thought about that as I leaned on the car, watching traffic, watching the numbers on the pump tick upwards. The sun was already bright, and I was glad to have my sunshades.

By the time the pump clicked off, Tara was back at my side.

She said the station had coffee, but only small cups.

We stood there, staring at traffic as if a major decision was to be made.

"I need a large," I said, after thinking about it. "For the road."

She agreed, and we left without coffee.

We didn't get far before the two of us decided we

were hungry, too. Tara spotted a diner and we pulled in. The parking lot was full, so we created our own space at the end of a row of cars and hoped we wouldn't get towed. It was a *no parking* zone, but we were all about making our own rules. The world was our sandbox and we were building castles. Plus, the books were selling, and we had money. We were living the dream, and that dream included parking, sanctioned or otherwise.

The dream, however, did not include a diner so crowded we couldn't get through the front door. We stood deliberating, looking through the glass at the back view of a bald man in a plaid shirt.

"Let's just drive," I said. "We'll find something."

So we drove. We had been awake for over an hour without our morning cups. Back home it was a ritual: I would wake early, start the coffee, and begin writing. Tara would wake later, but once she was up she would start in on the coffee with me. Then it was coffee all day. That was how we operated, full steam ahead. Without coffee, we didn't know what might happen.

We took Midkiff to I-20 and headed east. There was nothing on the service road, so we took an exit and got on a big four-lane heading back into the city. We saw a coffee shop, but it was on the wrong side of the median.

"If we don't find something, we'll circle back," I told her.

We found a deli just down the road and stopped. We were the only customers and the two girls behind the counter weren't too happy to see us. One had brown hair and wore a lot of makeup. The other was rail-thin and couldn't stop scratching her neck.

The first thing I asked was, "Do you have coffee?"

"Well," the thin girl said, glancing at a coffee pot

beside the soda fountain. "Yeah."

But she drew out the *yeah*.

Yeah, but there's none made.

Yeah, but I don't feel like making any.

Yeah, but when I do make some it won't be any good.

So much conveyed with that one word.

The two girls shared a quiet, subtle laugh amongst themselves.

"We'll just have water," I told them.

We ordered our sandwiches and watched as the girls assembled them. Slowly.

We ate at a little booth by a big glass window and talked about how well the signing had gone. We talked about the book festival in Austin in October. We talked about the next book and our next move.

Then we talked about how nice it would be to finally get some coffee.

There were no other cars at the coffee shop. None in the lot, none in the line. We pulled up to the board and eyed the menu.

Then we noticed a hand-written sign taped next to the speaker.

Brewer's broken.

No coffee.

We exchanged a glance. Then I leaned out the window.

"No coffee?" I asked.

"No sir," said a voice; male. It crackled through the speaker.

I exchanged another glance with Tara. She snarled, then leaned toward the window, shouting, "Why are you open, then?"

"We have muffins," the guy said.

"But no coffee?"

"No coffee."

I settled back behind the wheel, drumming my fingers on the armrest. Then we drove around the building.

I put the car in park and we idled. The situation was getting desperate. It was almost noon, and still no morning cups.

"I guess we just drive," I said.

Tara rubbed her temples.

"I'm going to get a migraine if we don't find some coffee soon," she said.

"I know."

I pulled the car onto the four-lane and headed for the interstate.

Just as we passed beneath a bridge, Tara's hand shot out. She was pointing.

"There's a *Stripes*!"

Stripes is a brand of service station. You see a lot of them in West Texas. We had gotten good coffee from *Stripes* before.

"Last chance," I said, crossing traffic to get to the parking lot.

Inside we found a coffee station. Spigots, and cups, and creamers, and straws. Wadded up coffee napkins at the foot of the trashcan and coffee rings on the counter top. I grabbed a large cup, held it under the spigot, and pulled the lever.

Nothing.

"Are you serious?" Tara said. "You've got to be freaking kidding me."

I could see the potential for a fit in her eyes, brewing like a storm. Brewing like the coffee should have been. She was dangerously gorgeous in that moment; A brooding thundercloud poised to erupt in wild, irrepressible torrents.

And then came our saving grace: A small Hispanic woman with short gray hair and a grandmotherly smile.

"I make some," she said in broken English. "Sit. Sit. I make some."

Moving quickly and with purpose, she ushered us to a small table nearby. We sat and thanked her. Then we watched as she replaced filters and filled them with fresh grounds.

Soon we could hear the coffee brewing. After a while, we could smell it.

And not long after that, we were on the road again.

"You know how I feel right now?" Tara asked.

We were eating up miles. Eating them up and washing them down with fresh, bold, and deliciously fragrant coffee.

"Content?" I guessed.

"Better than content," she said. "I feel *capable*."

"Of what?" I asked.

She had this look, the impish smirk of someone who is resolute, defiant, and just a little mischievous.

"Everything," she said.

We drove, enjoying our morning cups in the bright, hot sunshine of mid-afternoon.

Capable, I thought, as we rolled toward our next adventure.

About the Author

SJ Duncan is an author, ghostwriter, public speaker, and musician. He collects old typewriters, dabbles in photography, and was once a member of a CCR tribute band. He lives in North Texas with his wife, children, dog, and the old typewriters.

For more information visit
www.sjduncan.com